W9-AGI-725

Setting Boundaries

Learning about Healthy Relationships

BY ALYSSA KREKELBERG

The Child's World®
childsworld.com

Published by The Child's World®
1980 Lookout Drive • Mankato, MN 56003-1705
800-599-READ • www.childsworld.com

Photographs ©: iStockphoto, cover, 1, 5, 6, 9, 10, 13, 14; KK Tan/Shutterstock Images, 17, 18, 21

ISBN 9781503844575 (Reinforced Library Binding)
ISBN 9781503846722 (Portable Document Format)
ISBN 9781503847910 (Online Multi-user eBook)
LCCN 2019956606

Printed in the United States of America

ABOUT THE AUTHOR

Alyssa Krekelberg is a children's book editor and author. She lives in Minnesota with her hyper husky.

Contents

CHAPTER ONE

Being Comfortable

Zach leans in to hug his friend, Rachel. But Rachel does not hug him back. Instead, she frowns and pulls away from him. She looks upset.

Zach is **confused**. He and Rachel are not fighting. He asks her what is wrong.

It is important to pay attention to how people show their emotions.

By hugging someone, you can get into that person's personal space.

"I do not like hugs. They make me **uncomfortable**," Rachel says.

Zach thinks about what Rachel said. He likes hugs. But he can understand why someone might not like them.

Zach asks Rachel if they can fist bump instead. She smiles and agrees. Then both friends are happy.

THINK ABOUT IT!

Has one of your friends ever made you feel uncomfortable? How did you tell him or her about it?

Why is it important to understand how your friends are feeling?

Friends can help each other be comfortable together.

You may feel lonely if you do not have anyone to play with at recess.

CHAPTER TWO

Needing a Friend

Lea does not have anyone to play with at recess. She wants to have fun. So she sits on a special bench. It is called a buddy bench. Kids sit on this bench when they are **lonely**.

Ross and Jamie do not know Lea. But Ross sees that Lea sitting alone on the buddy bench. Ross knows that he would feel sad if he was in Lea's shoes.

Ross thinks about what he would want to happen if he was on the buddy bench. He would want someone to come up to him and ask him to play.

If you think about how other people feel, you can find a way to help them.

You can have fun playing with new friends.

"Would you like to play with us?" Ross asks.

"We want to play with bubbles," Jamie says.

Lea smiles. She loves bubbles! She is glad that Ross and Jamie noticed her on the buddy bench. They have a fun time together.

CHAPTER THREE

Stop and Think

Sarah is watching cartoons on the computer. But her sister Lin wants to play a board game with Sarah instead.

"That does not sound fun," Sarah says. She moves the computer away. Lin starts crying.

Sometimes people want to do different things. That is OK.

A compromise is a good way to make both people happy.

18

Sarah knows that Lin is upset. She could play a board game with Lin to make her feel better. But Sarah does not want to do that. She tries to think of a **compromise**.

"I do not want to play a board game right now," Sarah says. "Can we play a game on the computer instead?"

Lin smiles. She says that she was lonely playing by herself. But playing a game on the computer sounds fun, too!

Sarah moves the computer so that both of them can see the screen. By finding a compromise, Sarah works on a healthy relationship with her sister.

Friends and family members can have healthy relationships with each other.

GLOSSARY

compromise (KOM-pruh-mize) A compromise is when you agree to something that is not exactly what you wanted, but meets some of the wants of others, too. Sarah found a compromise with her sister.

confused (kuhn-FYOOZD) If people are puzzled or unsure of something, they are confused. Zach was confused about Rachel's actions.

lonely (LOHN-lee) Lonely means to be apart from others and miss their company. Lea felt lonely, so she sat on the buddy bench.

uncomfortable (uhn-KUHM-fur-tuh-bull) If someone is not relaxed or is in discomfort, they are uncomfortable. Rachel was uncomfortable with getting a hug.

TO LEARN MORE

Books

Kreul, Holde. *My Feelings and Me.*
New York, NY: Skyhorse Publishing, 2018.

Merk, T. M. *Painting a Peaceful Picture:*
Respecting Peers. Mankato, MN:
The Child's World, 2019.

Smith, Bryan. *What Were You Thinking?*
A Story about Learning to Control Your Impulses.
Boys Town, NE: Boys Town Press, 2016.

Websites

Visit our website for links about healthy relationships:
childsworld.com/links

Note to Parents, Teachers, and Librarians: We routinely verify our Web links to make
sure they are safe and active sites. So encourage your readers to check them out!

INDEX